where *the* apple falls *: poems*

where
the apple
falls*:poems*

SAMIYA BASHIR

⊕REDBONE PRESS

WASHINGTON, DC
www.redbonepress.com

®REDBONE PRESS

P.O. Box 15571
Washington, DC 20003

ISBN 0-9656659-7-6
Printed in the U.S.A.

Cover art © Ruth McFarlane
Cover design by Eunice Corbin
Author photo © Sophia Wallace

www.redbonepress.com

Acknowledgments

Poems from this collection originally appeared, some in slightly different form, in the following publications: *Bum Rush the Page: A Def Poetry Jam; Cave Canem #7; Obsidian III; Role Call: A Generational Anthology of Social & Political Literature & Art;* and *Arise.*

I would like to acknowledge and thank the Astraea Foundation, Poets & Writers, and Cave Canem for their generous support in the completion of this work.

Notes

Firefox is a Kwansaba, an African-American poetic form, created and used by poets Eugene Redmond and Amiri Baraka.

Other Books by Samiya Bashir

Best Black Women's Erotica 2
(ed.)

Role Call: A Generational Anthology of Social & Political Black Literature & Art
(co-editor with Tony Medina and Quraysh Ali Lansana)

American Visa
(limited edition chapbook)

Wearing Shorts on the First Day of Spring
(limited edition chapbook)

for Hazel

Deeper still, between girls
under fathoms of water,
blind plants and a litter of
fish heads,
deeper, still deeper, among
clouds once again
        you come flying.

—*Pablo Neruda*

I know that I am shaking you,
that I am twisting a knife in a wound
hardly healed; but what can I do?
I cannot help remembering
in my forced solitude and reclusion.
—*Mariama Bâ*

Contents

Moon Cycling
Sankofa Speaks

Don't come in my house woman
Smellin' all warm like that
Please   if you know
What's good for both of us

Don't come by my door
Smellin' fresh like that
Sizzling like summer
Steak   medium rare
I'll think you are
My supper

Don't ignite my passion
Get my taste buds swole
Get me so I've got to have
Some of what you are
Offering   You are offering

Take care
With what you put
On my plate   place at my door
Where you stand when you know
I'm licking my lips
Scratching my nose
Jumping on one foot
Ear to the door
Listening

I.

Of Saints and Suppers

for Alexie & Jeffers

I.

Shiny white patent leather shoes.
Topped with glimmering buckles.

Starched crinolines.
Steam-ironed, handmade matching sister dresses.
Although preacher say Jesus don't like vanity.

Aromatically fried hair.
Curled to patch burgundy burn marks:
hot combs, cigarettes.

Dirty white tights worn under
ruffled, Temple-ish girl pants.
Both clean when we dressed.

Exhaustion.
Monotony.
Grumbling stomachs.
Peppermint candy!

But what of transmogrified bread,
holy, crumbling crackers,
grape juice in tiny glasses,
misunderstood prayers of
temporary redemption?

The interminable wait
for the call to commune
with Jesus at the snack bar
mama often chose salvation over breakfast
never as long as the patience needed
to sit quietly, digesting deliverance,
fidgetless, bicker-free
before a slow recessional into the sunshine.

II.

Can I find my liberation in bread?
Must it be white? Wheat? Wonderous?

Can that bread be attached to pizza?
No pepperoni? No sausage?

Can I make a sandwich?
Say, salmon, just to hedge my bets?

Could I, perhaps, bake a cake?
Pound, bundt, layer?

Do I really even need this body,
if I have a whole bottle of blood?

III.

It took me a decade to purchase
this microwave oven.
I hope Jesus doesn't mind
radiated flesh from time to time.

I use it to stack my deck,
when I need a quick-save.
Blood curdles.
Flesh burns swiftly.

Oh, Lord!
Why have you chosen bread over chicken?
I wish to taste you in most anything.

Oh, Lord!
Why have you forsaken ice cream?
How can I teach the children
of your sacrifice, without it?

Oh, Lord!
How can a crusty old cracker compare
to crisply baked macaroni and cheese?
Perhaps you were trying to
help me watch my weight?

Oh, Lord!
Do the vampirical undead eat bread?
Can I slide by on a bottle of beer?
A few glasses of wine?

IV.

The recession
My mother, children in tow,
stands desperate on a Saturday afternoon
forced to choose between day-old bread,
and a jug of wine.

This week we can be only half-saved.
We must mind our Ps and our Qs.

My arms are growing tired,
waiting for her decision.
I mistakenly ask her,
little-girl lisp on high:
Which
is the matter?

Toward the Coming Night

Hennaed fingers push the carpet open:
First the berry red
      Then the midnight blue
      The eggshell border marked with ink
      The color of her mother's lamb stew
Stomach growled its readiness
To break the long days fasting
      Left knee crouching
      On a leaf spray of green
      Right knee pressed
      Into an orange sunset
Hands and feet ashy
Blame arctic water washing
Sandpaper throat too parched to speak
Crooked back bowed into the new black moon
The creak of tired bones cautiously hidden
In the ochre cushion of a moonlit oasis palm

Nature Rising

1.

May flora fawns all over herself.
June steams cold limbs awake, coaxes into birth.
July sets aflame all that once rested damp, wet, willing.
August stretches scorched like a desert caravan calling
September rains desperate still to quench this thirst.

2.

amber moon wanes
in the cornflower sky

losing fullness like
a hysterical pregnancy

regular intervals set your
clock predictability

tomorrow's ambassador passing
through yesterday's land

gathering fullness again
each time a broken promise

3.

God's eyelid lifts
bats a windy eyelash
at the new day

growing broad
bright demanding
feeling itself turn on

another new day
electric orange sparks
misty greetings

love juice flowing vast
as seven seas exposing
last night's landlocked love

rivers stroke delicate curves
lake ripples lap shoreline lips
all night by this waning light

4.

in full midday light
secrets run and hide
like stovetop roaches
cursing lost crumbs

rough sticky irresistible
clarity's candor calls you
in dares you to reveal
intention motivation action

driven to summertime excess
bold flowers charm honeybees inside
loud like 125th street hair queens
know everybody needs to get some

before winter this light their only hope
reproduction not even the point
just being touched squeezed taken
serious needs require this action

while visibility is high
drunk on self recognition
delirium does its job raising
temperatures to fever pitch

5.

dusk creeps in
a soft surprise
met with moans
and sighs lulling closure
to noontime braggadocio

days work almost done
consummation awaited
by shallow bated breaths
slow shedding of intimate
barriers nature rising to task

that nosy big bellied moon
creeps over the horizon
illuminating everyone's business
like neighbors keeping fence builder's
family fed   projecting her own

lamentable condition
up and down up and down
forced to face another crisp
hot cheeked sorrow borne
with each miscarriage

calls herself shedding light
aiding completion of this
necessary task copulation
moisturized seed spreading
to wax dimming into dawn

Blue Light Basements

1.

when i grow up
i wanna be like traci

wanna huff and puff like her
wanna move and writhe
be tiny and throw-around-able
like her   yeah like her   always
smiling no matter what's in her mouth
no one telling her not to talk with it full

she can say   whatever she wants
to anyone   do whatever
and everybody   likes to kiss her and stuff
i know   i've seen it

close enough any
way up late
at night i watch her move
practice that pouty grin pretend
someone wants me for it
someone wants it   when i grow up
someone wants me   i try it out a lot

get used to how it's gonna feel
i don't wanna look like a fool
show them that it hurts
but it's hard to get the pout right
sometimes   that hurting part is distracting

2.

the details: turn volume down, sit arms length from screen,
never lose access to *STOP, PAUSE, REWIND*, attune every fiber,
nerve, single sprouting hair, to slightest sound, movement in the
house, breath. learn to put things back precisely as found, fast
forward through the money shot.

know the order by heart: get on knees and suck dick, spread legs
for awkward tongue stabbing several seconds long. he fucks you
this way. he fucks you that way. you moan. make noise or don't.
writhe, slither, or not. groan, shiver, sigh until it's time.

act surprised by the sudden jerk: back on your knees, suck,
maybe pump, maybe lick until it happens. take a breath.
prepare to erase any trace of yourself and retreat.

3.

and the half-spilled tumblers dot every cabinet.

each drawer holds hidden bottles. cans.
every crevice of the house keeps secrets.

pile of debris knows well enough:
stay silent about the late night that left you
untended, vulnerable to the quickstep crush.

4.

the classics: vanessa; marilyn. certain role models. late nights at
the basement wet bar before the big screen. girls stretched reel-
to-reel to album to videocassette to the 1 to the 0. class, right? left
beside the carcasses of after-work martinis, the leavings of young

couples with excellent carriage. on the flip side, hooked. hang out
at the video gallery; wait for customers to leave. try to find a clean
entrance beyond the velvet curtain. everyone inside invisible,
fixing like rubber tube to bicep. beyond permission.

sprint through years of wanting: gray basement hiding, liquor
smoke drinking, shades drawn like surprise at the sudden jerk
coming – on cue – from above, practice moves no desire remains
to use, shirk discovery. distract from the hurting. wait for the kiss.

At the Altar

Rubber gloves, cotton mitts,
sweat coats brow, sprinkles lips.
Reach up for the kiss.

Stole the pink plastic cup
from the clinic kiddie corner;
used the enema tube bought
at the 99-cent supermarket.

Sometimes it's best fresh,
sometimes frozen.

Younger brother has
much to give, needs
minimal notice.

Want to moan, raise hips
to meet hand, reach into
forests of hair, whisper.

Fight the urge to run back
into the wardrobe, cower
behind denims and silks.

Reach down for the kiss;
close lips around communion.
Wait for answered prayers.

Angel Gets a Witness

1.

Born in the year of the fourth coming
of Christ, Angel missed Armageddon by a hair
and an err in mathematics. Mother hoped

Angel would rise higher than the rest.
She studied with the passion of Abraham,
sought the perfection of Isaac until glory

proved so damned elusive. It seemed no one she loved
could be saved. If Christ had returned as ether
this time, his tour bus missed Los Angeles.

2.

Angel awoke deep into a helpless night
rushed to Mt. Sinai, to find her brother risen
blood red shirt soaked through, an accident

in a sea of crisp blue. Such sartorial laziness
led to deadly result in this harsh, desert landscape
The introduction of six crippling shots ended

argument. Angel had believed in her brother's
temple as proof of the righteousness of her own.
This was when it all began to fade to black.

3.

Angel anointed herself twice daily, filled and drained each bath midway
through, feared her own overabsorption. She scrubbed away passion
with persimmon seeds, drank coconut milk to douse any leftover flames.

On alternate days she flushed her insides with rosewater. Her temple was
tight, fine, but never seemed to get clean enough. Only 144,000 chances
at a mercy she gave up at that crackling bus stop. Instead she took up

smoking, drinking, loving with abandon. Angel loved Marcus
in public, Mary in secret, shoved watchtower prophets into
shallow closets, drew blinds to block their insistent light.

4.

Ever brighter, Angel chose her own governance, burned
incense and poured libation down her throat. Climbed ever higher
seeking prophecy in an ever-changing truth. Reached as far as her

neatly clipped nails could touch, ran bruised fingertips over her closely
cropped head, gazed into the eyes of the sun, weighed heaven against
earthly paradise, measured them both against the joys of the wicked.

Angel made her choice, climbed to the tower's pinnacle, treading each
flight with the lightest of fearful steps, brought bright, colorful balloons
to illuminate her journey, turned her back on mercy and leapt.

Core

She would never be questioned
were it not for the apple in her throat;
asked to verify herself, explain the easy
mistake she made while still in-utero.

To her it has always been plain,
a process of continual unlearning,
mirror to millions of unfolding moments
each fifth blossom petal endures, alone,
before summer scorches finality into branch.

She blamed her mother, in part,
who carried layers into bone the faith
that manhood was easy; socked away
in nightly prayers and daily wishes for
a child to be born correctly, all the right equipment
placed to wrestle the world to the ground, pin it
despite its will, without worry for the sweeping silk
gathered before a squat.

Even then she listened;
willed her own ovaries to form and drop,
encouraged her nourishing nipples to dry out
their ducts, pressed for the playground privilege
pecs afford, traded size for certain strength,
acknowledged Y as subject.

From the first surprise smack
she realized her mistake, screamed

burning cries for return, the chance
to make another choice.

Still, the seed took root. Remained.
Each promise she'd made bore fruit,
bounced its affirmation at her throat,
betrayed her, announced her fall,
face forward and in profile. A question
marked swallow hungry for an answer.

Clitigation

Her Opening Argument:

> I am nature
> rosebud, tadpole,
> cumquat, sweet
> fruit of an ever
> ripening tree.
> Would you leave
> my branches empty?
>
> Has man's palate
> so soured he is willing
> to live on bark and
> blade and rotting meat
> with nothing sweet
> to cleanse him?
>
> I make things bearable.
> Slight nub rubbing to
> welcome you to this world
> even before the hands.
>
> Leave me be
> and I can put a smile
> on an old woman's
> wizened face—teach
> a young girl the art
> of teaching herself.

Witness One: Sara Jane Pitt, age 10, Rides the School Bus

Whooo-Wee!
hope they don't
nevah nevah
pave these old roads.

I been takin my seat
in the back now for
one full year, sit
alone if i can,
position my seams
tight over the right
spot—just so—

I ain't been late
to school once.

Witness Two: The Lips of Her Lover

She taught me the art
of craft, of perfecting
technique / made me
a passable kisser. Brought
the two corners of my
meeting up closer to
my eyes when I
hear her sighs.

I wrap her like a
gift, enclose her like
night to starlight cover

her in her nesting
place like I was
a mother hen / her
my chick.

This miss done brought
my self to my self
taught me how to
shut up and just listen
to love, showed me
like a tuning fork
how to feel sound.

Without her I could still
feed. I could still sing,
but there would be
no worthwhile songs,
nothing succulent enough
to entice me to open the
tongue's route to taste.

Witness Three: The Lips of Her Self

Ma lady she keeps me full,
gimme sump'n ta hol' onta,
caress on the cold nights
we lie alone together.

She is my timbre,
carries the weight
of my pitch, floats

my notes on her back
conducts my lyric
/ treble to bass /
needs no instrument
but the hood that
keeps her warm.

That ol' shawl she
be wearin like ol'
grandmamma spider
waxin on her web
make 'er look proud,
when really / still /
she be so, so humble.
I alone / 'cept maybe for
the rivers she commences
to flow / can enter beneath
her shelter unbidden, pop
in for a mid-day tea,
set-n-chat a while.

We was made
together / like two
spirit eggs. I stand
here today and hold
ma sista's hand,
refusing—i said
refusing this
separation.

(Having learned to ignore the prosecutor's nonsense,
our lady diligently prepares her closing.)

Still / The Crossings:

Don't you feel empty
Aunty?
Didn't you scream?
Wasn't that shard of
some old master's looking
glass far too unclean?

Didn't you bleed
for weeks?
Didn't your mother,
your own aunties
have to hold you
down hold you down?

Didn't you want to
run when this thing
was done to you—
you—who stand
with my accusers?

Didn't you cry all that
night—and all the
next and the next
in your mother's own
weeping arms on
the days after the
last you truly trusted
her?

And you / lover /
do you warm to her
even as she turns away
in shame? Don't you
want her to love you
back / move with you /
meet your moans
with her own?

Tell the people how
you must hold her
as she shakes at
night! Tell them how
this woman you love /
you love / has eyes
that go empty with
old, old fright!
Tell us how she
winces in pain
after all these
years. Be honest,
don't you miss your
lover's laughter?

    Crossing Mama:

    whyi yi yi yi yi yi ?????????
    !?!?!?!?!?!?!?!?!?!!!!!!!!?????
    !!!!!! How could you to me how
    could you to me your own
    baby girl your own baby—
    mama—how could you?

Where is your memory?

Have you lived so long
with your own heart
closed that you think
nothing of shutting
my door? After
birthing me, were you
in so much pain
you could not let me
live? Mama?

Mamamamamamamamamamama mama ma
You saw the rusted tin
the blood soaked
ground i was placed
on, you knew the
pain i was in like
your own and still
you held me / down /
down / down / down /
down.

You cannot tell me
you've forgotten the
taste of dirty cloth
blocking your screams.

You dare not say
here in fronta alla
dese folks that this

oft-cursed tradition
was worth so many
years of these bitter
rock hard salty
tears—mama?

Mama—why do you
hate us both so?

In Closing:

So you see
I am not for ground
spilling / thorn stitching
was not formed
for even cold
anesthetic
cuttings / as if I
were some dis-
placed fern or
bougainvillea.

I speak in whispers
and song. I am
eucalyptus, soothing
a wheezing chest;
orange sun rays
warming mercury
reaching even the
farthest plutonian
moon.

I am birth
and the access
to birth, love's
sheltered throughway,
tropical rain and the
noontime humidity it
washes.

Pass through me /
dark to light /
wash over me
with rivers of joy
embrace me with
your love—if I'll
have you—but know
I am no one's for
the taking. No—
I am not even mine
for the taking.

II.

Power

what are you waiting for?

bath drawn
coffee warm
eggs scrambled
poached and
fried over easy

the baby has been fed
changed, oiled, powdered,
sung to read to put to bed

lawn mowed
homework done
living room tidied
floors mopped
tabletops dusted

the car was gassed last night,
fluids checked, windshield wiped,
green tree hung from mirror

skin lotioned
nails clipped
lips lined
hair washed
combed and oiled

work clothes have been ironed
for the morning, shoes shined,
train fare in your pocket

wine poured
sofa pillows fluffed
jazz on the player
with rhythm and blues
doing doo-wop back up

the court, your court, where the ball lies inert
has been swept clean, net tightened,
bugs brushed off, night lights amped

but the gas needs flame to burn,
the match needs sulfur to strike,
the pot of water needs fire
to steam   what's cooking
sits at simmer, ready to boil.

blood & wine

my cries sampled on FM radio
the wai-wai-wicki-wailing at
the walls built up around my heart
an unnatural protection

my nails scratch
at packed tight masonry bricks
i didn't know i could build

it becomes harder to distinguish
between the free and plenty samples
and the costly real deal

i don't know if i'm crying
or if i've cut to commercial

concentrate

there is a fresh water pond
where i wash my hands and feet
cover my head and shoulders
before i kneel

there are grooves
worn places where my fists
assume their position
regularly—i know this place well

wai-wai-wicki-wailing at my wall

the echo of the auction block
driving me mad
the proctors & the gamblers sell
my sorrow back to me

the drumbeat
of my own highly pressurized heart in the
background, my own brother giving the pitch
at such an incredibly low price
i can hardly wai-wai-wicki-wait
to go in and buy it

quick fix distraction from my cry
waiting on the rainbow takes patience
a certain faith that tears can be filtered
through mortar and bricks
a certain trust that will keep me from running
to the store cash in hand
knowing if someone is selling my pain
in one aisle
they must sell some relief
in the next

Mustang Sally

rode her steed
best she knew how

side saddle
backwards
breach

more often though
than not
she was ridden

hard steady swift
like December morning
breaths—in and

out of the lungs—pushed
into low hanging
frost bitten skies

steam ordered into
water lockstepped
into ice hydro-

planing in plain
view of everyone
she knew

when Sally rode
she broke barriers
of sound, branch and

twig, murder and that
place, that place that
hovers just before murder.

Sally held herself tighter
than a tumbler of gin, drove
whatever she rode like

there was no
tomorrow hoped
that there wasn't

and when Sally tore through
town like her virgin dressing
gown the folk just shook

their heads side to side, sucked
their teeth, whispered poo-pooery
none too silently

never once warning her
to slow down.

Gwendolyn's Attic

handmade jumpers   for mama's first step   twirling
batons and foreign coins which cling to carpetbags   the
patch stripes from Stratford's old brown mess hall uniform
Mattie's hand loomed threads still peeking   through
Sunday dresses and Friday night shoes   stocking patch kit
in case rationing reclaims the order of that   bright red
change purse in the corner by the shoebox albums of sepia
photos   the sounds of Sapora's naughty laugh   Epreval's
Pullman cap plate   hand bleached nursing uniforms
stethoscopes   shopping bags from the old Hudson's
department store still filled with receipts for easy exchange
and return   the ribbons the baby used to fly around
the world   patent leather shoes from the 1,956th
celebration of boulder moving flight taking   Gussie's
loving kick in the pants   Aileen's joyous cackle
Eleanor's blue eyed grin   the scent of Annie Noble's
tobacco   the silent pain Eliza carried that Black woman's
alchemy she used to love Willie despite his white man's
nose   the angular curve of his fingertips   in the corner
by the peephole window sit clumps of Alabama clay   minds
eye movies of barefoot summers   sharp dressing Detroit
nights   Amy's ballet slippers hang next to   Gloria's
dressing oil   and Pamela's stitch books the fifth set of
keys to that old Chevy Nova   Socrates' collar and
games for long summer nights   when Brett's laughter
would fill up the basement and Harriet's wild explorations
concluded   with hugs and kisses   lifted from
that old Negro   hymn book

Floating Down the Delaware

Leaves of three thrust vain, shiny
skins upward, past the intrusion,

trying to shed light on the matter.
Black skin rots cerulean blue. The

two bodies were found on Thursday
night. No wonder I can't keep track

of time. It was just Thursday yesterday, last
week, about a month ago, and now—same

newspaper, usual pen, overpriced corn flakes
in a bowl, another concerned look spreading

lines across my face, running late. I wouldn't say
that all black people know each other, but I knew

these two well enough. That bridge under which
they swept still haunts, takes ages for me to cross.

Stuck Up That Mountain

me and that deer
this spider those
fireflies over there that
pregnant moon smoking clouds
this coatblanket these swollen
feet up in the airy ceiling of
pennsylvania trying to get some-

where just like the skunk whose
unsuccessful attempt to cross
the street left him up here
with that carpet of trees

and that blank empty
cut out part in the middle
with no trees just stories
of slicing these rubber tire shreds
this dark windy silence

and flora and fauna and bird
song and that drop
of water from that
waterfall and that other
one and that other

one time was you could
see clear through to the ocean
from here could smell that vapor

dewy humid sky rising from the
crater lake sat below time
was now just sitting alone
running polluted exhausted so many
strangers can't find nothing but junk
food—cheezits and puff pastries
sodapop and shit—too tired to read too
rapt to strike this match hit the power

switch turn on anything can't walk
away no room to move all that's left
is sitting at the back of this bus ether
and ethanol in equal amounts breath

American Visa

This country is my co-dependent enabler.
The wife who hides my bottles, gives
credible excuses to my boss and children.
She steamrolls through my consciousness,
seeps in through unguarded gates,
lies prostrate, flipping the channels
of my attention repeatedly
back to an esteem seeking self.

She is not the victim here.

My compliance leaves plenty
of damning, forensic evidence.
She calls the extra rolls of flesh
at my sides (front/back) love handles,
brazenly flaunts a lack of knowledge
of the world outside of herself,
sends me to duel with
my own cavalier attitude,
sits a six shooter solidly
on each plus-sized flank.

Milady faithfully tells me
my station, where I can
get off, and with whom.
She mispronounces my name
out of habit, an arrogant judge
of my phonetic compass, and

thrusts her own miscalibrated
needle in my face, handing out
directions like one tourist who
thinks she's helping another.

On Moving On

Our entanglement twists
winding around poles labeled
rent, utilities, dinner with your family.

Taut, high-strung fiber-optic wires
communicate mutual consent
personal lament—it's too soon.
It's not soon enough.

I began labeling records and books
between trips to the country. Things
were all we could hold separate then.

Slowly the sofa became mine, lamps
and candles yours. You kept
movequickables, lightbrightables,
memories that fit in your pocket.

You carried the night sky's eagle
further north. I held fast to her swan.

Narcissus Sits by the River
to Take the S.A.T.

Two brains leave their stations
at the same time, headed toward each other
with matching speeds. Sparks will fly
when they crash into each other.

Yes, fatalities occur.
They carry biological entities
that will change the ecosystems of each
and the point of meeting forever.

Does this new life with no name that they create
belong to a recognizable genus/species?
If it's not easily categorized, should they kill it?
Mark it as an historical find?

At the river's edge rest No. 2 pencils.
Erasers. From the forest's farthest end
wafts a drumbeat—a resistance song.
From the moss patch at his feet the timer ticks.

To the Moon

For the sake of argument, I will
marry a young Indian woman,
a pacifist warrior
with the best hair oil
in the county.

This is not a literal declaration.

I am attempting to sleep with
enough white women to equal
-10^3 as many white women
as all the players of the NBA
in all of the years of its existence
including the old times when
white players ruled.

I may mean none of this.

I intend to be taken care of
by elder black women
all of my live long days because
doesn't everyone?

I have always been a good American m'atriot.

Still, I have no plans to nurture
anyone. I may never secure
another's fears in the warm
embrace of my too-soft arms

I see no children suckling from
these abundant breasts
those whose howls are quieted
by the rocking of my shoulders
or the slow back and forth
of my lap under their bellies
will by most accounts
remain incidental.

But I will demand;
That is for certain.

I will scream for my own nurturance.
I will howl my personal pain.
I have every intention of screeching
my loneliness to the stars like radio waves
bouncing from galaxy to galaxy
until they reach back to the indigenous
times and the indigenous people
of the firmest terra of my birth
and between the oceans of this impending death
when the waves of my torturous sadness
pass through these narcissistic strands
that reach from the roots of my scalp
to the ends of the universe in search
of the perfect anointing oil,
a salve, a marriage bond
tying me from head to feet to heart
to the moon and back to who I am
to who I was to however
I may possibly be loved.

Where the Apple Falls

Where latitude stretches compass into quiver
her wise branches rest before crawling into bloom.

Sharpedged, tight fisted buds lead the way
from dormancy to the first blush of untrusting
blossom, white with fear of discovery.
Each process begins anew, though roots run
long, deep and generational, winding through
underground rivers when rainfall fails to quench.

Emboldened by her growing audience
of bees and snacking weevils, hostelling
bluejays slapping five with vociferous,
red breasted robins, each flower spins
her tale. She is griot, having dreamt her
songs through snow covered nights,
she wakes to make love to a seeking sun
before her visitors come.

They anticipate every punch line,
tickle her with stinger and claw, peck
for each bit she drips into eager beaks,
rubs between stomach and feet.

When her labor is at its peak she draws pilgrims
from every direction. Some come with baskets
wrapped in soft hands, folded skirts, strong,
leaning backs. Others bring axes and blades.

The first fruit is promised before birth, its branches
tied with sweet butter ribbon. The rest hang heavy
on her chest, growing plump, syrup and pulp pulling
taut skin against the cooling night. In turn, harvest
moon leaks gold in the swirling flush of dance aflame.

She needs this feeding, trepid, wanton lust. Each fruit
must be released. She pushes her story, note by note,
pitches crescendo to a rustling backbeat of wizened
harmonies. Everything that touched her took; her
song lies implanted, preparing to sleep, folded in
flesh of dreams, its next awakening already foretold.

III.

An Amazon's Confession

Yeah / i sold da man
he was tryin to cut me
up / tie me down / beat
me into serving his goats
and bearing his chirren /
i only bear mine

got de idea from dem
very men / carrying rows
of dem selves to de wata
ta put on da big ships
an' carry away

thought dem funny looking
men wit no sun in dey skin
an' de loud killin sticks dat
spray fyah would carry dem
off / make me rid of de mess
wit de knives and de obeyances

take 'em way
make 'em wear all dose
piles a clo's when de sun
is de closest and walk
how dey feet don' nevah
touch de groun' / yeah

i sold 'em.
got me some grain
an' some buildin' tings

for alla ma sissas
to remake our village
thicker, fortified an'
strong / keep dem mens
from tryin ta carry us
'way to be goat wives
an' ting

wasn't 'till I meet da man on da
udda side de ocean
i start to tink
mebbe udda way

almos' wanna laugh
ta see him goat wife to de
man wit no sun in his skin
an' de loud killing sticks
almos' wanna laugh

cuz still he looking at me
like he doin' ma job
cuz when dat man wit
no sun come from makin
me bear his chirren / still
he looking at me like

/ we
all stuck doin my job
an' all dem fire stick
holdas done somehow
only robbed da man a his
for short time

Walk on the Water

Featherstep dragonfly shooflyshoe.
Lightheart salmonleap waitingbear dodge.
Dryeyed postsigh morningscalenoslippers.

Armswing synchronicity. Chinup.
Lookahead sunrayriding ripplesail faith.

Move.

Through Tenement Window

Caught: garbage and gates.
Dense, midday fumes exhaust. There!
A dove finds relief.

Bronco Busting

wild mare reared up
felt the smoke rise
from deep within
each nostril flaring
into flame

all around her sat chains
linked fences to keep her
hemmed in   a tether
lay in wait at the center
of her runaround pen

at the door of the gate
cowfolk rested in wait
of her decision   will
she run fight dodge
settle or lay down
easily broken

she never agreed
on the catching
the too small coffles
which bound her
kept her from
wild fields where
choosing lay
with her mood

they sent in dogs
to sway her
bend her to their work
bow her down
for their branding but

no animal could refuse
the swish of her tail
the majesty of her mane
the sparkle of freedom
in her eyes reminded
them of their own / instead

as cowfolk entered
weapons drawn determined
to make her decision
for her the dogs turned tail
bared teeth to their masters
took guard of the gate
and like Oya's rancorous wind
she ran

Reach

I touch my toes,
Reach down past
Obvious places
Toward exposure,
Stretch defenseless,
Finger my way into the carpet fibers
To pull soft inner spaces open for you.

Because when you call me *Baby*,
I keep firm grasp on the woman
You speak to when you say, *All right
Babygirl, it's time to say good night.*

Because when you call me *Beautiful*,
I embrace it like a flower girl, drop petals
To guide you to the bouquet.

When you say *yes,*
I say *please;*
When you say *no,*
I thank you.

Even now, I reach down,
Let soft breeze cool my hot spots,
Allow for condensation, even now
When more than fingers grasp long
Knitted strands, even now, when
Delicacy turns breathless, yes, even
Now, I remember my manners.

Want List

—after A. Matejka

Seedless watermelons whole;
heavy as a 10-month baby,
juicy as her after birth.

I want to feel sugared flesh drip
from the upturned corners of my lips
freed from the spitting of wasted seed.

Or, rather, to become the oft-sown earth;
to feel like a fifth generation field
bursting with nutrients, bearing cornstalks
the crows fly over with reverence,
black heads bowed to their flaxen flames.

Still,
I need to be pecked, tapped
like the old-growth maple sap
in some remembered sacred forest,
its sticky syrup served with Sunday breakfast.

Sliding down poles like a latex dancer
I yearn for slick waterslides instead.
Immersed in a cool public pool
I raise red chlorinate eyes toward the sun,
contemplate its heat as reflected by
last night's moon bath, wonder if these planets
that sustain me stand alone between the two.

In mid-day I want a nap.
At night I want hands and reach,
by morning my desires stretch
to arms, to shoulders. I dream
of neck twisting, of the last curl
at the tip of each lock.

At the moment of gestation
when the fetus makes the choice
to remain woman or become man,
I want a raison d'être printed across
the rounded belly.

If not,
then what I need are choices,
available options, shoes to grow into
and jeans that shrink to fit and stretch
back out again so I can walk in comfort,
with minimal distraction, at my own pace
between these amaranthine destinations.

The Mayor on the A Train

Deep, long and winding—
Reminds him of a pasture
he can almost smell.

A Train Answers Back

Emergency brake
Titillates, swings and sways.
Teasing. Whispering. Pull!

What I Can Not Do

And yet I can not undo a bomb's detonation
can not piece together bits of bone and flesh
resurrect some beloved spirit blown apart.

I know no way to separate the mushroom
from the cloud, the firing pin from the trigger, but
I can separate the napalm from the hand that sprays.

I'd like to create a new multiplication table
where 7 and 3 have roots squared and whole;
where zero is not ignored or assumed.

My new math created, I would order new calculations
of the death tolls of yesterday's wars, insist they are used
to halt the killing tomorrow, place a moratorium
on the fighting for the counting day.

If I could, I would sit on the cold auction-house floor
before Picasso's painted ladies, separate the pink-
fleshed paint into decisive reds and whites, add water
and oil, add blue, add green, emulsify into my mother's face
before the pain. But I can do this

no more than I can return to her womb, separate
the cells of my embryonic self into egg, into seed.
I can not go back and offer her young body
the freedom to choose my birth. For her I would
do this: dismantle my flesh as I would not
dismantle my spirit. This is what it tells me:

I can not quiet the warrior's midnight screams.
I can not give oxygen to the soldiers buried alive
in desert sand; I can not sit idly by while my back
yard becomes Guantanamo, my living room imprisons
for profit. I can not convince children to go gentle

into good night dreams if I can not disarm
the bogeymen reaching out to frighten them
from every screen. I can not answer the cancer
which grows like pigweed carried from new world to old.

Some things I must sit with. Some things I must ignore.
some things I hear on the radio while making love,
while others I must implore my neighbors help for.

And yet I can not undo a bomb's detonation
nor piece together bits of bone and flesh to
resurrect some beloved spirit blown apart.

I know no way to separate the mushroom
from the cloud, the firing pin from the trigger, but
with furious fingers I yearn to stop the bullet.

Foxfire
—for Baraka

Dodging compass: Preface ravages pouting warpoem queries.
Ecstasy excuses nocturn soldier bullets. (Perhaps, Songman.)
Riotous sunsets quieted raucous, enraged, phlegmy baboons;
Rageful redbone breasts sparring flushed, fruited nipples.
Inquire, bloated coondog! Pioneer spectre! (Fawning zealots!)
Embrace smoking rhythms, warring, spastic, saltine sonnets.
Recover; betwixt devious haunted castles: Phoenix demurs.

Hush, Fire. Hush.

Just because Khadijah
was a bread winner,
truth sayer, baby maker
wound healer, home maker,
care taker, high profile CEO,
strong sister from around the way,
backbone of modern faith, we must
never speak of her.

If we choose to
she shall be called
wife.
Second party to;
guest list plus one.

Simply because it was her Visa
that got maxed out all the way
to Mecca and back, because her
labored breathing bore daughters
and sons, because her shoulders bore
so much weight and her mind held the key
to the livelihoods of generations hence
she shall remain a background player.
A bit part. Best, in fact, played on stage
by young boys. Unschooled is preferable.

There can be allowed
no imagination of her
in the fullness of her reality.

This is why burnings are required.
It is best, pupils, if we close our eyes to her:
selling her wares in markets
all over town, her team
if marketers ever loyal,
trusting her to return to them
their due amount; keeping tabs
of business both at home and abroad
while her other half prayed and preached;
shaking her head yet again
while the obvious was explained
to the barely willing
in the carnivorous
circles of men.

Yes, she worshipped.
She was alive, wasn't she?
Passionately so. There were things
She never needed him to explain to her.
It was part of their bond,
this knowing. Some days
she loved his infinite patience.
Some days she just wanted him
to show up for his shift.
She knew God's work was
important as well as she knew
that feeding her children was God's work.

There were evenings
she shook her covered locks
as she gazed on their gatherings

so filled with ecstatic grappling
for a light so blinding she wanted to laugh,
wondering to herself which
of their heads were harder.

Yet, every morning, like the moon
bowing with graceful deference
to the burning sun, she ensured
the cakes were on the table,
ready to be dipped in honey.
Each afternoon she supervised
The bathing as she counted
the days receipts. Every night
she suffered with her husband
the frustrations of offering guidance.
Her arms were ever open. Her arms
were ever open. That is all
that is safe to recall.

The Trouble with This Harvest Time

he says i like it rough
and i do   i do
but that's not the point

the point is i don't
know him didn't invite him
in here didn't ask for him
to come don't want this

it is true
i go looking
for trouble

i often step in piss
and don't wipe my feet
at my own front door

i wait for red lights
before cross walking

i stroll deserted streets
in short tight skirts
high heels made for
not-running clicking
the announcement of
my solitary arrival

it is true
i don't wait

until spoken to
before i speak

and my tongue
trips over native
idioms speaking in
itself when probing
stranger flesh

yet
each time i light a cigarette
i pray that it won't kill me

yet
i fight addiction's
red caped seduction
one handed with plastic
straws tiny mirrors and
promises so many promises

in the subway station
alone at night
having slept through
the safety of daylight
i stand on edge contemplate
the closeness of that third rail
catcall scurrying rodents
clicking   clicking

i wait for blizzards
and oil slicked highways
to drive too far too fast

and sometimes
i'll eat pork chops
in the afternoon laughing
in the face of december's
crescent moon

and sometimes
i'll kneel on a mat
swallow deep
nag champa breaths
and fall dead asleep

i've walked past
al-anon meetings
to get to the irish pub
all alone on a paycheck
friday in south boston

and yes, i keep sharpened razors
near the bathtub spigot just in case

and yes, i have swallowed
the barrel of a gun
but i never buy bullets
never   it is true

i go looking
for trouble struggle
with the grown up
concept that these things
come any other way

but rough   i do
i do   but

that's not the point
i don't know him
didn't invite him in

didn't ask for him
to come here don't
want this   not this
still

Having it All

The so many bills
The nonstop shrill of
The telephone the cat
Fights my headache

Virtual mail
Cyberchats uploading
Downloading due
Yesterday yelling

At those cats kids
Neighbors friends
Lovers corner-store-men
Smelling putrid litter

Garbage piss
Poverty fried
Anything rotting
Everything

Short days
Shorter nights
Long hot marches
Heavy packs
Upwards upwards
Always higher mountains
Shoeheels higher still

Death Toll

An Affirmation

I made it. I crossed over
every bridge without jumping,
waited for green light each time
before running into traffic,
swallowed no gun barrels, drew
no bloody baths, swung from no
trees without a seat attached.

Didn't take anyone with me.

Almost can't believe I'm lying here:
my kids and their tag-along therapists
sitting nearby in tears with no thoughts
of their monetary inheritance, trying
to block out even their spiritual one,
wanting to keep me with them one
more day.

Verbose as ever, but my mouth is dry,
I've been ready for decades, I say,
But I'm glad to have had until today.

My partner holds my hand and my
lovers send cards out of respect.
She douses my forehead with
magnolia water, dots my lips
with rosehip kisses. Often shushed
grannies pull my toes, ask when we
can play their favorite game again.

I tell them: *Tomorrow, my sweets.*
Tomorrow we'll play.

About the Author

Samiya Bashir is the editor of *Best Black Women's Erotica 2* and co-editor of *Role Call: A Generational Anthology of Social & Political Black Literature & Art*. She is the author of two chapbook poetry collections: *Wearing Shorts on the First Day of Spring* and *American Visa*. Her poetry, stories, articles, essays and editorial work have been featured in numerous publications including: *Bum Rush the Page: A Def Poetry Jam; Obsidian III; Cave Canem #7; Kuumba #4; Poetry For The People: A Revolutionary Blueprint; Contemporary American Women Poets; Best Lesbian Erotica 03; The San Francisco Bay Guardian; Ms. Magazine; Black Issues Book Review Curve; Vibe; Seventeen; XXL; Lambda Book Report;* and *The American Journal of Public Health*. Bashir is a fellow with the Cave Canem: African-American Poetry Workshop and a founding organizer of Fire & Ink: Writer's Festival for LGBT Writers of African Descent. Her work has been reprinted internationally and she has read her poetry to audiences across the U.S. and in Europe. Bashir has won numerous awards for her poetry since serving as Poet Laureate of the University of California during her studies, and continues to teach creative writing to adults and children.

Other titles from RedBone Press include:

does your mama know? An Anthology of Black Lesbian
Coming Out Stories, ed. by Lisa C. Moore
(ISBN 0-9656659-0-9) / $19.95

the bull-jean stories, by Sharon Bridgforth
(ISBN 0-9656659-1-7) / $12.00

the bull-jean stories (Audio CD), by Sharon Bridgforth
(ISBN 0-9656659-2-5) / $12.99

last rights, by Marvin K. White
(ISBN 0-9656659-4-1) / $14.00

nothin' ugly fly, by Marvin K. White
(ISBN 0-9656659-5-X) / $14.00

love conjure/blues, by Sharon Bridgforth
(ISBN 0-9656659-6-8) / $14.00

Spirited: Affirming the Soul and Black Gay/Lesbian Identity,
ed. by G. Winston James and Lisa C. Moore
(ISBN 0-9656659-3-3) / $16.95

You can buy RedBone Press titles at your local independent
bookseller, or order them directly from the publisher
(RedBone Press, P.O. Box 15571, Washington, DC 20003).

*Please include $2.50 shipping for the first book and $1.00
for each additional book.*